The Trading Bible

Trading Made Simple: Understanding ... ETFS and Forex ...

By Kiril Valtchev

Copyright 2016
All Rights Reserved

The Trading Bible®

Trading Made Simple: Understanding Futures, Stocks, Option, ETFS and Forex

By Kiril Valtchev

TABLE OF CONTENTS

Conclusion

DISCLAIMER

The Trading Bible is for educational use only. Stocks, Futures, options, and spot currency trading have large potential rewards, but also large potential risk. You must be aware of the risks and be willing to accept them in order to invest in the futures, foreign exchange and options markets. Don't trade with money you can't afford to lose. This book is neither a solicitation nor an offer to Buy/Sell futures, spot forex, cfd's, options or other financial products. No representation is being made that any account will or is likely to achieve profits or losses similar to those discussed in any material on this website. The past performance of any trading system or methodology is not necessarily indicative of future results. For the avoidance of any doubt, the Trading Bible and any associated companies, or employees, do not hold themselves out as Commodity Trading Advisors ("CTAs"). Given this representation, all information and material provided by the Trading Bible and any associated companies, or employees, is for educational purposes only and should not be considered specific investment advice.

Introduction

So you want to learn about trading. I salute you. Trading can be one of the most financially rewarding professions around. There is no other profession around like trading. It can also break down your character, scatter your blood pressure and leave you completely broke. The good news is, through careful research, relentless work ethic and adjustable plans, trading is a tamable beast. In order to succeed in trading you have to begin to develop a strong thirst for information and knowledge.

It begins by carefully conducting an honest self- assessment. Knowing what is expected and being able to shift your attitude and work ethic so you can be prepared to handle brutal market moves. Losses are, and will always be a part of trading. So being able to limit them without going completely insane is key. By having the sufficient capital that you are not afraid to lose will help ensure your trading is more smooth and controlled.

It's not always good to be in the market or in a trade. Understanding how, why, and when the market moves will make you aware of when to avoid trading. Knowing basic market functionality from simple concepts to complex market orders can help you gain an edge in the long run.

Solid liquidity, low-costs, and speed are essential to being a quick and efficient trader. It is vital to understand the best securities to trade and where to trade them. All financial instruments trade differently and sometimes they flow together. Seeing how instruments behave during different times will help you see their predictability.

Will there be a new paradigm for trading within the next few years? With the evolutionary changes in market technology every day, people can't argue with the fact that markets are indeed evolving by the second. Technology that was once available to only exchanges and institutional traders is now at the fingertips of anyone with enough funds to open a trading account.

Powerful computers, internet faster than the blink of an eye, electronic markets and direct access trading have made trading possible for more people than ever before.

This book is meant for anyone who has ever had a strong interest in trading. From beginner to expert, this book aims to go through the depth of financial markets in order to help you understand how markets behave and to hone your own personal trading strategy.

Markets will fall and markets will rise, it is within their very nature. Prepare yourself by learning all there is to know about the markets. Equip yourself with the full and complete knowledge of the markets before you decide trading is for you.

CHAPTER 1

Brief History of Trading

In 1791 the first stock exchange was established in Philly, the leader in foreign and domestic trade. In March of 1972, twenty- four of New York City's main merchants met in secret at Corre's Hotel to create a systematic way to bring order to the securities exchange business and rip it from their competitors, the auctioneers. Two months later they signed a document called the Buttonwood Agreement named after their original meeting place, a buttonwood tree, this agreement started the New York Stock & Exchange Board. In 1863 it would get its name snipped to the "New York Stock Exchange".

The agreement had two major provisions. Brokers were to exclusively deal with each other, which would eliminate the need for petty auctioneers. The commissions would be set at .25%. In the beginning, government securities formed the basis of the early trading. Later on, bank and insurance company stocks added to the volume of transactions. The stock market began to expand as the country started to become more industrialized. Additional exchanges were later created during the Civil War, one of them being the American Stock Exchange.

Trading has been around for more than a century. Today we are reliant on technology, but the idea of buying and selling stock by the public has been around since the late years of the 19th century. Small businesses were created in big cities across the country which would allow people to make **"plays"** or **"trades"** in the market. These became known as **"bucket shops"**. Players, or now modernly known as traders, would contribute money in the common **"bucket"**. The money was then used as security for purchasing stocks or commodities with leverage. This enabled small traders to speculate on stocks.

The action in bucket shops was pure madness. A clerk would read the ticker tape while another clerk wrote prices on a chalkboard, almost like a game. The traders or **"speculators"** were able to quickly buy and sell the stocks as the **"ticker"** was read. Money was won or lost based on the honesty of the shop operators. Needless to say majority of bucket shops were unlicensed and illegal. Bucket shops were crushed with the Stock Market Crash of 1929.

Today's major exchanges include The New York Stock Exchange (NYSE- the Big Board), American Stock Exchange (Amex- part of NASDAQ), Pacific Stock Exchange (PSE), Philadelphia Stock Exchange (PHLX), Chicago Board of Trade (CBOT), and the National Association of Securities Dealers Automated Quotation system (NASDAQ). Foreign exchanges include Germany (DAX), France (CAC), Hong Kong (Hang Seng), Japan(Nikkei), and London (FTSE). Exchanges collect fees for each share that changes hands by utilizing its services.

So how is a market created? It's really not as difficult as you may think. A market is created when similar items are traded and exchanged. Any type of market is the gathering of willing buyers and sellers. The purpose is to create a network on which they can trade across. Trading in the stock market is just the transfer of money of a particular stock or security from one willing buyer to another willing seller. This requires both sides to agree on a specific price.

The Crash of 1929

October 29th, 1929, commonly known as the Great Crash, or the Stock Market Crash of 1929, was the biggest stock market crash in the history of the United States. It sparked the beginning of the Great Depression. On October 29th, 1929 **("Black Tuesday")**, over 16 million shares switched hands on the NYSE.

Billions of dollars were lost which ended up crushing thousands of investors. The volume was so high that stock ticker prices ran behind because the machinery at that time could not handle the massive volume of trading. Some stocks actually had no buyers at any price that day. Due to the irregular volume of shares traded that day, the ticker did not stop running until about 7:45 p.m.

On the next page you will see the drastic fall in the stock market during that time.

Crash of 1929

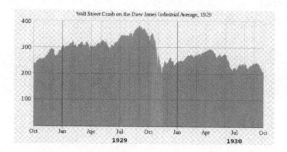

Stock prices had nowhere to go but up in the weeks following the crash and there was considerable bounce back in the following weeks. Even though there was a minor uptick following the crash, prices continued to slowly drop as the US spiraled into the Great Depression. By 1932, stocks were only worth about 20% of their value in 1929.

The crash was not the only cause of the Great Depression, but was the main factor in accelerating a global financial collapse. By 1933, half of the US banks had failed and unemployment was approaching over 14 million, or roughly 30% of the workforce.

US REGULATORY COMMISSION

As a result of the crash the Security and Exchange Commission (SEC) instituted regulations to ensure that another crash would not happen. Congress created the U.S. regulatory commission in 1934 after the Senate Committee on Banking and Currency investigated the NYSE's operations during the crash.

The purpose of the commission was to aid in restoring investor confidence by ending bad sales practices and stock manipulation tactics that led to the collapse of the stock market in 1929.

Provisions of Committee

- Prohibited buying securities without adequate funds to pay for them

- Provided registration and supervision of securities markets and stockbrokers
- Established rules for solicitation of proxies
- Prevented unfair use of non-public information in stock trading
- Stipulated that a company offering securities is required to provide disclosure of all information

NASDAQ

In 1971, the National Association of Securities Dealers (NASD) created a fully computerized and integrated system called the **NASDAQ** (National Association of Securities Dealers Automated Quotation system). It was the world's first electronic stock market. In the beginning it was only used as a quotation system and there wasn't a way to perform electronic trades.

This allowed NASD members to post competing bids and offers on a number of stocks electronically .The NASDAQ helped lower spreads on stocks. Needless to say many brokerages were not a fan of this because this is where they made most of their money. This essentially led to the creation of the OTC market.

OTC Market

OTC stands for **Over-The -Counter**. Trading on the OTC market is done without the direct supervision of an exchange, therefore there is an overall lack of transparency. It is commonly referred to as a **"decentralized market"**. The market is for securities or derivatives that are not listed on a regular exchange. The major reason that an instrument or security is traded on the OTC market is because the company is very small and can't meet the capital requirements set by a regular exchange in order to get listed.

Securities are commonly known as **"unlisted"** because they are traded by broker dealers. The broker dealers negotiate directly with each other over the computer or phone. OTC securities trade on Over the Counter Bulletin Board (OTCBB) or more commonly known as the pink sheets. Most of the time these are penny stocks.

Penny stocks tend to be pretty dangerous and manipulated. They can be fake companies or companies with terrible credit ratings that are trading more on hype than anything else. In general there is an overall negative connotation with regards to penny stocks. In reality not all penny stocks are bad news. Some companies are just in their starting stage and can't meet the standard demands set by the regular exchanges in order to get listed.

The 1990's: The Rise of Online Trading

From 1996 to 1999 online trading began to explode as technology and internet traffic began to drastically increase. Average Joe's now had the opportunity to trade on the same real-time pricing as most brokers. This is where the day trader was born. So what are some of the things that made all this possible?

- The rise in tech stocks created massive market interest
- A massive drop in commissions and fees from the standard broker model
- Improvements in computer processing
- Higher trading volumes and easier access to wider competitive pricing
- The rise of online brokerages like TD-Ameritrade and E-trade

The rise in technology and investing helped to push employment, productivity and wage growth to new highs in the 1990's through the end of 2000. There was a dramatic rise in 401(k)'s and mutual funds.

Over this 10 year period productivity rose at 2.2% annual rate, real wages averaged 1.3% a year and unemployment fell below 5%. Online trading continued to evolve and a new era of high- frequency trading and algorithms took hold.

The Trading Frenzy Today

Online trading today is easier than ever before. The drop in commissions and fees over the years have made trading more attractive to everyone. It was reported that the number of brokerages increased from 12 in 1995 to more than 130 by the end of 2000. This widespread increase in brokerages gave birth to high-frequency and algorithmic trading.

High frequency trading is done at speeds that can't be seen by the naked eye. It involves specialized computers, specialized order types and order routing functions with the focus of only being in the market for a very short period of time. The goal is to to capture tiny profits thousands of times within the course of a day.

High frequency trading has been happening since around 1999 but the speed was nowhere near where it is today. Orders would take several seconds to fill and now execution has decreased to unfathomable speeds of milliseconds to even microseconds.

Many people argue that this new form of high frequency and algorithmic trading poses new threats to the overall structure and functionality of the financial markets. There are many cases to support that this is true and many that will argue against it. One thing that we can't deny is that trading has become more accessible to the general public in a much more cost effective way than ever before.

As speed and overall trading costs continue to improve we will continue to see a dynamic shift in how trading is done. The evolution of trading has and will continue to change our lives and the structure of how money is transferred and valued.

CHAPTER 2

TRADING VS. TRADITIONAL INVESTING

Before beginning to trade it is very important to make the clear distinction between trading and the traditional style of investing. This will determine if trading is for you. Trading is definitely not for everyone but anyone willing to continuously learn and apply themselves will achieve results.

DAY TRADING

You have most likely seen the sketchy and annoying ads about how a genius day trader turned a small amount of money into millions in a very short period of time, and now for the first time he will share his secret trading strategies to the public.

You never get to hear this so called **"secret strategy"** until you actually buy what the advertisement is selling. Most of the time the costs are in the thousands. The cold hard truth is there isn't a secret strategy that exists for day trading. The market is going to move no matter what. The best strategy is the one that is constantly adjusted based on market trends in order to minimize your downside and maximize your upside.

Day trading is about price action and how you can effectively position yourself to hop on short price moves for quick money. Day traders care about low cost trading instruments, great liquidity and laser fast execution. They rely more on technical factors and news events that can move the price of an instrument rather than fundamentals, even though fundamentals do matter. They tend to have a preset profit target and set stop loss in order to limit losses and capture profit.

Day trades can be in a trade for a few days to a few minutes or even seconds. There is a multitude of different day traders. They span from MIT professors to the coked out Wall Street hot shots. They typically tend to fall into the category of retail traders or institutional traders. In day trading it is vital to understand the required character type, time, risk-tolerance, transaction costs and taxes in order to prevail.

Character Type

Day traders seek out volatility in instruments. The more volatility the bigger the potential profit but also bigger potential risk. This of course is not for everyone. You must be comfortable with risk and hone the ability to control your short term emotions. You must have an unbreakable character and allow yourself to be patient. Day traders must be quick to react when things go against them without losing an ounce of confidence. A master of action and reaction.

Time

Day trading is extremely time sensitive. A good trading day can be as short as a couple of hours or even a couple of minutes. Day traders can fire off hundreds of trades during a single session. You can be essentially glued to the computer screen waiting for the next price tick to come through to make your trading decision. You must be willing to spend hours upon hours to conduct research that will help you succeed.

Risk Tolerance

Day traders will try to make money regardless of where the market is. Successful day traders tame risk and are not scared to go long or short an instrument. Day traders can take multiple losses and profits within a given day as long as they are green at the end of the day. They are not afraid to leverage their positions to the max. As a day trader you can't just tolerate risk, you must learn to control it.

Transaction Costs & Taxes

Day trading can involve extremely high transactions costs. Typical retail brokers can charge you up to $10 a trade or even more. Average day traders can fire off 20 trades per day or more. 20 trades x $10 per trades is $200 in transactions costs in just one day. Imagine you did that every day for a year. The costs can be mind-blowing.

The tax implications on day trading profits are not that pretty either. Both day traders and investors pay taxes on capital gains. Capital gains are generated every time you make a profit for buying or selling a security. If you held a trading position for less than 365 days it's considered short-term capital gains. This is taxed as ordinary income.

Being aware of the required demands that trading brings will help determine if trading is indeed for you. It is definitely not for everyone. Knowing the demands that day trading brings before you decide to day trade is vital. It is also just as important to learn some of the basic and most common day trading styles.

TRADITIONAL INVESTING

Typical and traditional forms of investing emphasize around a similar strategy. The idea of traditional investing revolves around putting your money into safe assets and holding them for the long term to build wealth slowly over time. Some of these assets can include stocks, bonds, mutual funds and REIT's (Real Estate Investment Trusts).

As a traditional investor the investment that you end up selecting will depend on your long-term financial goals and what kind of market swings you are willing to tolerate. Below are some of the most common traditional investing strategies.

- **Buy and Hold** – This is the oldest strategy in the book. Buy and hold stock in companies which have solid fundamentals that have proven to be a safe investment in the past. The goal is to look for companies that pay solid and consistent dividends and hold them for the long term.

- **Contrarian Investing** - This strategy revolves around the idea of buying stock in a company during a down market year. Contrarian investors believe that during a down market year there are many opportunities to buy stocks in valuable companies at a considerable discount.

- **Value Investing** - Value investing is a strategy in which stocks are selected based on their intrinsic value. Investors look for stocks that they believe to be significantly undervalued based on a company's fundamentals such as current assets and earnings. Value investors can best be described as discount shoppers. The best real life example of a value investor is none other than the Oracle of Omaha, Warren Buffett.

You can't go into the world of trading or investing without hearing about the legendary investor Warren Buffett. With a staggering net worth of 65.9 billion as of 2016, you can't argue that Warren Buffett knows a thing or two when it comes to traditional investing. When asked how long his ideal holding period for a security is Warren Buffett responded, "Our favorite holding period is forever". He strongly believes that if a particular business performs well the stock will eventually follow.

One of his personal investing bibles he strongly advocates for and lives by is **"The Intelligent Investor"** by Benjamin Graham. He eats, sleeps and breathes the investment ideas outlined by Benjamin Graham. Buffett searches for businesses and companies that show strong signs of performing well in the long-term. He looks at management structure, functional operations, market dominance, consistent and sustainable profit margins. Investing with safety while minimizing the downside by searching for highly undervalued securities and instruments.

These concepts are very important for traditional investing and have made many of those who follow them extremely rich. Traditional investing can be a great way to build wealth over the long-term if you have proper patience, due diligence and a serious appetite for research.

These key points should now help you have a balanced understanding of the basic differences between trading and traditional investing. While both have the same end goal of making money they do it in a completely different manner. By conducting a careful assessment of your short-term and long-term financial goals you will be able to determine whether trading or traditional investing is the right option for you. There is nothing stopping you from making money day trading or investing slowly over the long term. Both methods have made many rich and can also do the same for you.

FUNDAMENTAL ANALYSIS

What is fundamental analysis? It is a way to simply evaluate a certain security or instrument to measure how valuable it is. In stocks, fundamental analysis focuses on analyzing a company's financial statements. By analyzing a company's assets, liabilities, earnings, management and competitors we can gain a better understanding of the overall health and value of a company. The main goal is to be able to gauge how a company will perform in the future. When fundamental analysis is applied to different instruments such as bonds, futures or forex, there is different data that is analyzed. Let's take a look the most important factors in fundamental analysis for stocks.

Fundamental analysis can best be split into qualitative and quantitative factors of a company. Both aim to get a better understanding of the overall value of the company.

Qualitative Analysis

Qualitative analysis focuses on analyzing management structure, cyclicality of the industry, a company's participation in unions, research and development departments and much more. It aims to get a better idea of the overall operational structure and flow of a company as a whole. Other qualitative factors can include the following below.

- Brand recognition
- Perception of management
- Customer experience and satisfaction
- Industry/competitive advantage
- Adaptability to change
- Track record
- Relationship with partner/parent companies
- Workplace culture
- Barriers to Entry

Investors like Warren Buffett become very familiar with the components above before deciding to invest in a company. Investors who plan to invest for the long term will also look at how employees feel about management and the company as a whole. Do they approve of the CEO, board members and current management styles? Sometimes it is not always easy to get answers to these kind of questions directly.

An investor can at least get some sort of idea about operations and management of a company through its **(MD&A)** section in the 10k filings. **MD&A** stands for **Management Discussion and Analysis.** This is part of the 10k in which you can get an idea of a company's operations and management structure. It essentially gives the management's opinion on current performance of a company and how it may perform in the future.

Quantitative Analysis

So what is quantitative analysis? Is it complex? Is it boring? Is it important? Will it make my head spin? The answer to all these questions is yes. For some it can be boring but for many it can provide the raw and unfiltered data that is needed to make an important investment decision. Quantitative analysis aims to look at the financial and business side of a company. It relies heavily on statistical models, financial statements, and economic data to make an investment decision. In the trading and investment community these types of people are often referred to as "**quantitative analysts**", or **"quants"** for short.

Financial analysis means everything for a company. It is used to evaluate budgets, current and future plans, employee-stock options, dividends, solvency and so much more. Let's dive into some of the basic and most commonly known financial analysis statements that are used by analysts every day.

Income Statements

The income statement is the holy grail of statements. It can often be referred to as a statement of income or profit and loss statement. Each geek has their own variation or version they like to nickname but for most it's just the income statement. It shows the profitability of a company during specific period, usually a quarter. The income statement along with all the others can be found in a company's annual report and 10-k. All publicly traded companies must submit a 10k the Securities and Exchange Commission (SEC) and release to the public.

Our analysts use income statements to get their beloved ratios to help them understand the company ever further. Analysts use performance, activity, financing and liquidity ratios to get a better idea of how a company's financial are doing. Let's take a look at some of the common ratios and stats that are used by analysts to understand a company's income relative to its expenses:

Performance Based Ratios

- ROA (Return on Assets)
- ROE (Return on Equity)
- EPS (Earnings Per Share)
- Profit Margin
- P/E Ratio
- Gross Profit Margin
- Dividend Payout Ratio
- Book Value Per Common Share

Activity Based Ratios

- Inventory Turnover
- Average Collection Period
- Asset Turnover

Financing Based Ratios

- Debt Ratio
- Debt/Equity Ratio

Liquidity Ratios

- Working Capital
- Interest Coverage

Balance Sheet

A balance sheet aims to show the company's assets, liabilities and shareholder's equity. A typical rule of thumb for the balance sheet is that assets must always equal liabilities plus shareholder's equity. The balance sheet is very important because it gives investors information about how much a company owns and how much a company owes.

Assets = Liabilities + Shareholder's Equity

On the next page are some examples of assets and liabilities that can be typically found in company.

Assets

- Cash and other cash equivalents (Cash, CD's, Bonds, etc.)
- Securities (Stocks, and debt securities)
- Accounts Receivable
- Current Inventory
- Prepaid Expenses

Liabilities

- Long term debt
- Bank loans
- Interest payable
- Taxes, rent, utilities,
- Current payable employee wages
- Customer pre-payments
- Payable Dividends

Statement of Cash Flows

The statement of cash flows shows the amount of cash that was made during a specific period of time. It tracks the amount of cash that comes into the company and the amount that leaves the company. The statement of cash flows can be divided into the three different categories below.

- Operating based activities
- Financing based activities
- Investing based activities

Operating based activities

Operating activities are direct activities that are involved with the business. This is typically the net changes in cash, accounts payable, accounts receivable, changes in inventory of the business and depreciation on assets.

Financing based activities

Financing activities involve changes in outstanding loans, dividend payments, issuing stocks or bonds. Majority of companies at one point or another will either acquire new debt, issue bonds, stocks and or dividend payments.

Investing based activities

Investing based activities can include purchasing new investments for the company, new equipment, real-estate, research and development. These are all essential to the stability and growth of all companies.

Qualitative and quantitative analysis are both important when evaluating the fundamental factors of an investment. Qualitative analysis values human capital and resources while quantitative analysis values statistics and direct finances. Both are crucial when deciding whether or not to invest in a particular security or instrument. By understanding both aspects in regards to how a company functions and performs investors can plan and make an intelligent investment decision.

TECHNICAL ANALYSIS

Since we now have a solid foundation of fundamental analysis, it is now time to enter the realm of technical analysis. Technical analysis focuses on forecasting the future price of security or instrument by studying previous price and volume movements. The goal of both fundamental and technical analysis is to forecast the future price of a security but technical analysis focuses on analyzing different factors that may affect the price of a security. The main focus for technical analysis begins with reading charts and indicators. Charts and indicators are the lifeline for technical analysis.

Technical analysts use a multitude of different chart and indicator setups to help them get a better idea of where price is heading. There are so many different indicators that an analyst can use and part of the reason is because anyone can create any custom indicator that they see fit. Below are the top 5 most commonly used technical indicators.

- Simple Moving Average
- Relative Strength Index
- MACD
- ADX
- Stochastic Oscillator

Each of the indicators above are powerful in terms of helping you forecast the future price of an instrument. Finding which one will be the best fit for you can depend a lot on what instrument you are currently analyzing.

Everybody has a different preference in terms of how they want to visualize the price of an instrument in order to gain a better understanding of its movements. In order to gain a better understanding of price behavior technical analysts need a proper chart setup.

Technical analysts love charts. They can use a variety of charts to gauge what is most likely to happen to the price of an instrument over a specific time. They can look at charts in the short-term, mid-term and long-term. Looking at each individually in relation to each other is key to understanding price. Below are the most common types of charts used by technical analysts.

- Line Charts
- Candlestick Charts
- OHLC Charts

What is great about charts is that they are highly customizable. There are a ton of different ways to visualize price when you combine different charts and indicators together. Charts and indicators are highly valuable tools to help you detect possible future price movements but it is important to note that they are not 100% exact.

You shouldn't rely solely on indicators and charts to get an idea of where price in certain instrument may go. It is very important to pay attention to what sort of news is coming out in the short term for a specific instrument. It is also very important to be aware when all markets open and close because price is a sensitive creature and has a chance to react during those times.

NEWS IN RELATION TO TRADING

Professional traders are very aware of when each market opens and closes. They are also extremely aware of upcoming news events that have a chance to move the price and volume of an instrument. Below are some common news trading events that professional traders take into consideration.

- Trade Balances
- Retail Sales
- CPI
- New Home Sales
- Durable Goods Orders
- Foreign Bond Investments
- Crude Oil Inventories
- Unemployment Claims
- GDP data

And perhaps the most important news event which happens the first Friday of every month is …….

- Non-Farm Employment Change

A full list of each trading day's upcoming new announcements can be found at the following websites below.

- http://www.forexfactory.com/
- http://www.fxstreet.com/economic-calendar
- http://www.bloomberg.com/markets/economic-calendar
- http://mam.econoday.com/
- https://biz.yahoo.com/c/e.html

Not every single news event will have a massive impact on the price movements of certain instruments. Some news events are instrument specific. For example, an earnings release for a certain stock or when a company goes ex-dividend. You can see when certain earnings will be released for a specific equity at the following websites below.

- http://www.nasdaq.com/earnings/earnings-calendar.aspx
- https://biz.yahoo.com/research/earncal/today.html
- http://www.morningstar.com/earnings/earnings-calendar.aspx
- http://www.marketwatch.com/tools/earningscalendar
- http://www.bloomberg.com/markets/earnings-calendar/us

Price is very sensitive to major news announcements and tends to move very quickly. Most news events will tend to have some sort of forecast in place by professional analysts. When that true data is released markets will react. If the data blows past expectations market moves will tend to be more dramatic. If the data meets the projected forecast the move will tend to be less dramatic.

Let's use the non-farm employment change as an example. The non-farm employment change, also known as non-farm payrolls, NFP and employment change, measures the change in number of employed people during the past month minus the farming industry. This data is released on the first Friday of every month.

Whenever this data is released there will be a forecast along with the previous month's data. Below are the following scenarios with different actual results.

- Good Effect = Actual Results > Forecast
- Bad Effect = Actual Results < Forecast
- Neutral= Actual Results = Forecast

So why should traders care? Trades care because this is a key indicator of how the overall stock market will move for the next following weeks or months. It can move at a slow and steady pace or a wild rollercoaster of ups and downs.

DIFFERENT MARKET OPENS & CLOSES

Prices don't just randomly move whenever they feel like it. There is a reason behind why a certain commodity price, stock price, or option price moves. For some instruments the majority of price movements can happen for only a two-hour period of the day. Some instruments can move around all day. By knowing when certain markets open and close traders can pick the most optimal time to trade.

There are times during the day in which prices move more often than others. As a trader you want to trade instruments in which there is good volatility, high liquidity and low spreads. Let's take the US market open for example. The NYSE and the NASDAQ open up at 9:30 a.m. and close at 4:30 p.m.

Depending on the day the most active time for trading the equities market is usually between 9:30 a.m. – 11:30 a.m., unless there is a planned earnings release for a specific company. Between 11:30 a.m. – 12:30 p.m. most traders, fund managers and institutional traders tend to go to lunch and volume tends to be lower. This is **NOT** always the case but typically the most active period for trading really only last for 2 hours or so. Imagine that, you can trade for 2 hours a day and do whatever you want for the rest of the day.

The link below gives you a full breakdown of session times for each specific market. Knowing when certain markets trade is key to becoming a top performing trader.

http://www.cmegroup.com/trading-hours.html

Price is the holy-grail of technical analysis. Being able to interpret it and makes sense of its behaviors will help you make smart trading decisions. Being able to make sense of price **and volume** will make you a consistently profitable trader.

VOLUME AND PRICE

Volume is a way to measure how much of certain instrument has traded during a period of time. Volume can drive prices up and down like a roller coaster. By understanding how volume is driving price up or down you can decide whether or not it's a good time to get into a specific trade. Volume can move due to some of the following factors below.

- Institutional buying
- News release
- Mergers & Acquisitions
- Support/Resistance prices

It is not always easy to identify why a certain instrument has moved up or down in price. In order to gain further details into the price action of a particular instrument traders can request an additional feed from their brokers known as Level 2 pricing. Depending on the broker you end up using Level 2 pricing can be provided to you for free. There are however brokers that will charge you a monthly fee in order to use it.

Level 2 pricing can provide you with tremendous information about the price action for a specific instrument. Level 2 pricing shows you the current orders that are changing hands for a specific instrument. It is most popular in equities but it is also used in futures, options and other products.

When an order is submitted it can be routed through different market makers. Level 2 displays a list of the current bid and ask prices from each market maker. By seeing how many orders are sitting on a specific price traders can get a better idea if that specific instrument has a chance to go to that price.

If you are going to be a serious trader you need to become an expert at reading Level 2 pricing. Level 2 pricing can paint a better picture of the current action behind the movement of an instrument. Below is a short list of things that Level 2 pricing can help traders identify.

- Current market orders that are pending execution on each side of the order book
- Analyze fast moving volume
- Identify low risk trading opportunities
- Identify algorithmic/institutional flow
- Highest bid prices, highest ask prices for an instrument

Below is an example of Level 2 pricing on an equity. On the left side you can Name, Bid and Size. On the right side you can see the Name, Ask and Size.

Level 2 Pricing

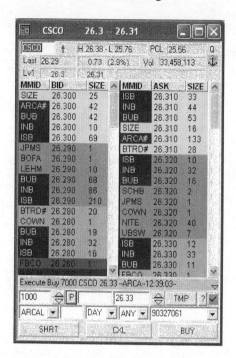

This is one of the most important tools traders use when day trading. It is essentially a cheat sheet to making profitable trades only if you take the time to fully learn all the ins and outs of its functionality. With Level 2 you can make sense of volume in relation to price and understand the dynamics of daily price fluctuations.

COMMON DAY TRADING STYLES

Everyone's style of trading will differ from one another because everyone has their own unique financial goals and appetite for risk. Some traders will want to make safe and calculated trades, while others will want to take the max risk to make the most money as quickly as possible. Below are some of the most common day trading methods.

- Swing Trading
- Scalping
- Arbitrage Trading

SWING TRADING

Swing trading is a strategy in which you hold a trade anywhere from several days to several weeks with the goal of profiting from a price change commonly known as price "swing". Traders look for forming price trends and trend breaks to get in a trade. Before a trend begins or ends there is typically a period of high volatility. Once that price volatility consolidates swing traders look to enter. They use a combination of technical analysis and some fundamental analysis to spot a good setup.

Methods to Learn on Swing Trading

A common assumption amongst swing traders is that **"The Trend is your Friend".** They attempt to place trades with the main trend of the market or particular security. If a certain instrument is in a downtrend the trader will go short. If a certain instrument is in an uptrend the trader will go long.

There aren't always obvious trends in price but there are times in which a particular instrument tends to move in a predicable manner between different price ranges. Prices in any security or instrument will tend to approach support and resistance levels.

If this is the case it can create swing trading opportunities. On the next page is an example of what a short swing trade and a long swing trade setup look like.

Short Swing Setup

In this example the stock price of ERTS (Electronic Arts Inc.) is an obvious down trend. The price temporarily reverts back up and then continuous on its way down. This isn't a big enough reversion in price to reverse the trend. This would be an optimal setup to enter into a short trade for 3-6 day period.

Long Swing Setup

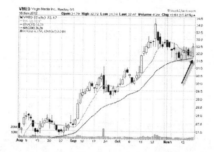

In this example the stock price of VMED (Virgin Media) is an obvious uptrend. The price comes down for a little bit and consolidates. There wasn't enough steam in the price to continue falling and it started to slowly move back up. This is an optimal setup to enter into a long trade on this stock for a 3-6 day period.

Financial instruments rarely move in a direct straight line but instead they can form price hopping patterns. Price might go up for a few days followed by a small pullback before going back up. Price can go down for a few days followed by small pullback before going back down again. There isn't always an obvious pattern formation. Understanding where key support and resistance levels are will help you avoid getting into bad trades even if the trend says to do so.

Support and Resistance Levels

A major element to technical analysis is being able to identify support and resistance levels in price. Support and resistance levels are the building blocks to day trading. They can come in many different forms and ranges depending on the specific trading instrument. Getting down the basics will help you understand where price has gone, where it has the possibility to go, and what price points you should avoid.

Support Level Price Explained

What is the support level price? It is the price level at which the demand for a certain security or instrument is perceived to be strong enough to prevent the price from going down any lower.

To explain further, if the price for a particular security or instrument begins to fall towards a particular level traders begin to buy more and sell less. When the price continues to get closer and closer to the support level the demand to buy will greatly outweigh the demand to sell and it will prevent the price from going lower.

There are of course times in which the support level will not always hold. Once this happens it means that traders have a stronger willingness to sell a certain security or instrument than they have to buy it. Once a support level breaks it means that traders are willing to sell at even lower prices which will inevitably establish a new low support level.

Visual Interpretation of a Support Level Price

In this example the support level price of Amazon (AMZN) looks to be right around $60 per share and the stock price has been staying above that since October. Support price is typically below the current market price of an instrument. Support level price is not 100% exact and it can be hard to always spot one.

Prices can move quickly and breach support levels temporarily and then revert right back up. Depending on the volatility of an instrument and pattern of behavior traders will establish price support zones and won't rely strictly on a particular support level. Traders may even wait for support levels to be broken for a certain period of time or a certain percent of the value of an instrument before deciding to enter into a trade. It is meant to serve as a cautionary level not as an exact determinant to enter into a trade.

Resistance Level Price Explained

So what is a resistance level price? It is essentially the opposite of a support level price. It represents the price level at which demand for a certain security or instrument is perceived to be strong enough to prevent the price from going up any higher.

To explain further, if the price for a particular security or instrument begins to rise towards a particular level traders begin to sell more and buy less. When the price continues to get closer and closer to the resistance level the demand to sell will greatly outweigh the demand to buy and it will prevent the price from going higher.

Obviously there are times in which the resistance level will not always hold. Once this happens it means that traders have a stronger willingness to buy a certain security or instrument than they have to sell it. Once a resistance level breaks it means that traders are willing to buy at even higher prices which will inevitably establish a new high resistance level.

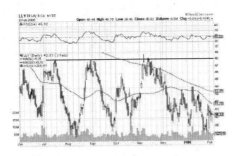

      In this example the resistance level price of Eli Lilly & Co. (LLY) looks to be right around $48 per share and the stock price has been staying below that since June. Resistance price is typically below the current market price of an instrument. Resistance level price is not 100% exact and it can be hard to always spot one.

Prices can move quickly and breach resistance levels temporarily and then revert right back down. Depending on the volatility of an instrument and pattern of behavior traders will establish price resistance zones and won't rely strictly on a particular resistance level.

Traders may even wait for resistance levels to be broken a certain period of time or a certain percent of the value of an instrument before deciding to enter into a trade. Just like a support level a resistance level is meant to serve as a cautionary level and not as an exact determinant to enter into a trade.

SCALPING

      What is scalping? It is a day trading strategy that focuses on making profits on small price changes throughout the day. Traders that scalp tend to place a lot of trades over the course of a regular trading day with the hope of capturing small profits over and over again.

Transactions costs can tend to run very high when scalping. Traders who scalp operate under the notion that they can limit their losses by being in the market for a very short period of time and their volume of small profits can amass to large gains over the course of a day, week or month. This can be true if scalpers implement a strategy that has solid stop loss rules.

The key component to being a profitable scalper is being highly conscious of spreads. If you can consistently overcome spreads you can be profitable. Generally scalpers will trade instruments that are highly liquid and have low spreads and transaction costs. The primary focus of scalpers is to make a small amount over the spread of the trade and then be out of the trade completely. This way they are limiting their risk and attempting to capture smaller market moves instead of chasing the big trades.

Scalpers also tend to look for brokers who offer rebate based volume trading or some sort of deposit bonus as an incentive. The goal for them is to churn high volume trades with minimal risk and essentially focus on making a ton of rebates. At this point it becomes a search for brokers that offer high incentives for volume. It becomes less of a market based trading strategy but it can still be profitable if executed correctly.

ARBITRAGE TRADING

Arbitrage trading can be the most complex and interesting style of trading. This is for the highly experienced and professional trader that has been in the industry for a long time. It is one of the most controversial styles of trading. There are books written solely about arbitrage trading and its implications on the market. For the sake of this book we will keep it short and highly interesting.

So what is arbitrage trading? It sounds complex and kind of dark. The whole idea of arbitrage trading revolves around the concept of a **"riskless"** or **"almost riskless"** trade. Arbitrage focuses on taking advantage of the mispricing of instruments and making a profit without any risk involved.

The goal is to capture profit on the disproportional pricing between two different markets or instruments. There are many advanced forms of arbitrage which require highly advanced algorithmic systems in order to implement. Let's take a look at some of the most common forms of arbitrage on the next page.

- Statistical Arbitrage
- Triangle Arbitrage
- Interest Rate Arbitrage
- Latency Arbitrage

Statistical Arbitrage

Even though this may seem like a complicated concept, statistical arbitrage is pretty straight forward. It involves the buying and selling of instruments based on their overall similarity. Sometimes the prices of instruments in a similar industry or sector will tend to follow one another. When the prices go out of sync it can create an arbitrage opportunity. In order to find possible trade setups traders look for instruments that are closely correlated or inversely correlated to each other. Let's take a look at the stock price of two companies in the same industry, Pepsico **(PEP)** and Coca-Cola **(KO)** .

Each bar in the chart represents 1 week.

We can see that for the most part these two companies have a high correlation to each other. Statistical arbitrage focuses on finding instances in which these two companies would go out of sync. Let's say for instances that these two companies on average are correlated at 75%.

A trader who focuses their primary strategy on statistical arbitrage would look for large variances out of this norm. If a trader noticed that their correlation dropped to 40%-50% for a certain period of time they might be inclined to enter into a trade.

The trade would include buying one security and short-selling the other. You are betting on the price of one security going up (the buy) and betting that the other will go down (the short). In this instance the trade you are in will be considered **"hedged"** or **"almost hedged"**.

The correlation between the two securities plays a huge role into this. Once the prices of the two securities start moving around, one position will make money and the other will lose money. The moment that one position is making more or significantly more than the other position is losing the trader can close their positions and realize the gain.

This is not a 100% fail-proof trading strategy. It is however a way to minimize the risk of a trade. It is very important that a trader is fully aware of correct correlation between the two securities prior to entering into a trade. It is also important that a trader is aware of the overall volatility of the two securities prior to getting into this type of trade. These kinds of strategies are deployed by some of the top trading hedge fund managers and institutional traders.

INTEREST RATE ARBITRAGE

This arbitrage strategy does have quite a bit of complexity built into it. So what is interest rate arbitrage? It is a trading strategy in which traders focus on profiting from the interest rate differences between two countries. This is typically accomplished by the use of a forward contract. A forward contract is a contract between two entities to buy or sell a specific asset at specified future time. We will use a more modern and applicable example to illustrate how this works.

This is most easily done and accomplished through the use of Forex brokers. This strategy also does carry risk depending on the broker. In forex or otherwise known as currency trading, traders can actually earn interest on trading positions that they keep open for every 24 hours. They can also be charged interest based on the trading positions they keep open.

This is commonly referred to as **swap interest**. On Wednesday's there is triple the interest paid out on specific currency pairs, otherwise known as triple swaps. There are brokers who offer swap free accounts and brokers who do not. The way this strategy can work for the modern trader is in the following way.

In order for this to work traders need to pick out a currency pair that pays traders interest. This can usually be found directly on the trader's platform. You should focus on picking currency pairs that pay the most interest. The direction of the trade will also make a difference whether or not you get paid interest or charged interest. This is very important. The following website below shows you how much you can make by holding a position open.

Forex Islamic trading accounts are always swap-free. They don't get charged swaps on open positions or overnight positions because it is against the Islamic faith.

https://www.oanda.com/forex-trading/analysis/financing-calculator

STEP 1) A trader opens up two different accounts with two separate forex brokers.

Broker 1: Offers **"Swap- Free"** Trading accounts. Interest is not charged or paid on holding positions.

Broker2: Regular Trading. Interest is paid and charged on open positions

Below is a list of brokers that offer swap free trading.

https://www.100forexbrokers.com/rollover-swap-free-accounts

STEP 2) A trader will choose a currency pair that pays out interest. For this example, let's use the AUD/CHF currency pair.

A trader will get **paid** swap interest by going **"long"** the AUD/CHF. A trader will get **charged** interest if they go **"short"**.

Let's take a look at an example payout.

Financing Calculator	USD
Account Currency	Trade
Interest Type	AUD/CHF
Currency Pair	0.74216
Trade Price(AUD/CHF)	1.02609
Current Price(CHF/USD)	0.76153
Action	Buy
Lend Rate %	0
Borrow Rate %	1
Number of Units	100,000
Hours Held	24
Interest Earned	$ 2.08

You can use this calculator at the following website.

https://www.oanda.com/forex-trading/analysis/financing-calculator

STEP 3) Open a long positions in AUD/CHF at the broker who pays interest and is not swap free. At the same time open a short position at the broker who does not charge swap interest. This hedges the two positions against each other and you will earn interest on one position without risk. Above is how much you would earn in daily interest for a standard 1 lot AUD/CHF position.

LATENCY ARBITRAGE

Latency arbitrage is also another advanced form of trading. It is something done by the best and fastest algorithmic traders. Almost all latency arbitrage is done through a pre-programmed high-frequency algorithm.

The fact is that different individual traders and institutional trading firms receive a plethora of different market data throughout different times of the day. This can create many instances throughout the day in which prices for securities from multiple data providers will be different. These are usually very quick and small price differences that are extremely difficult to see with the naked eye.

This can also occur when different data providers have small issues with their data feeds. If data feeds happen to get delayed for a specific data provider it can create the opportunity for latency arbitrage. A professional trader can see that the rate for a certain security is rising or falling much faster at one broker versus the other broker.

What the trader can do is program to buy or sell a certain security at one broker when the price at another is lagging behind and visa-versa. This can usually happen during news but it's usually extremely difficult to catch with the naked eye. Most traders that do latency arbitrage tend to have accounts with many different brokers. They also tend to have an external program built to aggregate all the data feeds into one. The trades are then programmed through each broker when price delays or major price differences occur throughout the day.

The key for latency arbitrage is speed. In order to have speed you need a carefully crafted and tested algorithm to execute these trades. These types of trades only tend to last for a few seconds and some even milliseconds. If a price feed gets delayed for more than 1 second latency arbitrage can happen without an issue.

The reason they are so common during news is because huge price differences are common amongst brokers during this time. There can be so many orders that are waiting for a fill during news time that the execution engine for the broker can get over-stuffed with orders and actually affect pricing.

This style of arbitrage is also not without risk. If your broker doesn't provide laser fast execution your order could get stuck and not execute properly. This can cause you to end up with a losing position. Knowing the risks involved with this style of trading is key. Below are just a few.

- Execution Slippage
- Delayed Order Fills
- Broker decides to wipe your trade
- Blacklisted IP

If brokers do not support this style of high-frequency trading they can decide to shut off your account and not have you as a customer. Before deciding to dive into this it is important to read the terms and conditions of each broker.

CHAPTER 3

STOCKS

Introduction

We have all heard of the term **"stocks"** being thrown around at one point or another in our lives. From the classic movies such as Wall Street to our friends, family and neighbors, stocks are one of the most popular investment tools of all time. Stocks can be one of the best financial instruments to create long term wealth. They are the building blocks to understanding our financial system. With the current advancements in technology it is now easier for people to own a small part in a publicly traded company.

There is no doubt that stocks are one of the most if not the most popular trading instrument around. People talk about them all the time as if they are experts but they don't know as much as they think they do.

What are Stocks?

In simple, a stock is a share in ownership of a public or private company. The stock of a company is divided into shares. A person who holds shares in a specific company is known as stockholder or shareholder. There are two types of stock: **common stock** and **preferred stock**.

Common Stock

When searching for what companies to invest in most of us will be buying common stock in the company. Common stock gives shareholders the right to participate in the growth of the company (appreciation in the price of the stock) and through dividends paid out to the shareholders. Depending on the state of the company dividend payments can change over time.

Owning common stock has its own unique rights. Common stock comes with **voting rights** that allow shareholders to vote on who gets elected on the board of directors or different company issues that may come up. This isn't always the same with every common stock so being aware of the specific class of shares you own is important.

Common stocks also have "**pre-emptive rights**". It gives the shareholder the right to maintain their percentage ownership in the company if the company decides to issue more shares. It gives them the right to buy a proportionate amount of shares in the company if there happens to be future issues of the stock. It is meant to prevent shareholders from getting diluted from their portion of ownership in the company. It is important because they protect shareholders from new shares possibly being issued at lower prices than the shareholders purchased them. They also incentivize companies to perform well so they can issue shares at higher prices.

Preferred Stock

Preferred stock differs from common stock in the fact that preferred stock often does not have direct voting rights. Preferred stockholders usually tend to have higher claims on company assets and earnings than common shareholders. Preferred stock typically comes with specific payment terms for dividend payments. They can be monthly, quarterly or annually depending on the structure.

The shareholders usually have first priority when dividend payments are to be made. They also have first priority in bankruptcy situations after creditors are paid. Preferred stock is actually listed separately from common stock and usually trades at a different price. Preferred stock has more flexibility than a regular common stock. It's important to read the terms and conditions of preferred stock before making a full decision to invest.

Sectors

Knowing the differences between common stock and preferred stock is important. The stock market is a wild animal. Knowing how this animal is structured can help you identify which stocks you should concentrate on trading. The stock market can be best split or categorized into different market sectors. Sectors are used to identify a section of the overall economy. By splitting the economy into parts we can analyze information specific to one industry or how one industry effects another. Below are the most commonly known sectors.

- Basic Materials
- Conglomerates

- Consumer Goods
- Financial
- Health
- Healthcare
- Industrial Goods
- Property
- Services
- Utilities

So how do traders and investors interpret sectors? Professional traders will tend to look at how all sectors performed on a weekly and monthly basis. This is where the core of their research begins. Traders and investors alike begin by analyzing which sectors are leading and which are falling behind. By seeing the performance from each individual sector in relation to all the others trades can begin to get a sense of the overall market movement. From here they can begin to dive deeper into individual equities.

Once you begin to understand how each sector tends to move the next step is to begin looking for individual stocks to trade within those sectors. You should focus on stocks that have the following criteria below.

- Trade above $3/ per share
- Have an average daily volume of at least 200k shares
- Have at least a 500 million dollar market cap

These are some pre-set filters that will help ensure that the stock has solid liquidity, low spreads and won't leave you with too much execution risk. Stocks that tend to trade below $3/share and have volumes lower than 200k shares are usually more volatile and very sensitive to huge news announcements. You want to trade stocks that have healthy volumes, mild volatility, and are well known in the marketplace.

Stocks that fall out of this criteria can also tend to have higher spreads which should be avoided as much as possible. Day traders are cost conscious creatures. The lower their overall trading costs the larger their net profit will be at the end of the day. Before placing a single stock trade you should already know that each trade you get into will always be a loser the moment you get into it. That is due to the costs involved. Below are the costs involved in a typical retail stock trade.

- Trade Costs
- Spread Costs
- ECN/routing costs
- Data feed costs/ Platform costs

TRADE COSTS

The only cost that is typically disclosed to traders when they are getting ready to open an account with a broker is the trade cost. The other two are typically left out. Most retail brokers will market their costs as $5-10 dollars per trade. There are other brokers that will give you discounts for doing higher volume on a monthly basis. Trade costs can be a flat rate or variable depending on your overall share volume.

SPREAD COSTS

The spread costs are going to be different depending on the stock you plan to trade. The higher the liquidity in a stock the lower the spread costs will be. Stocks with really good liquidity will tend to have a spread between .01 - .05. The spread cost is simply the difference between the bid and the ask price of a stock. Get used to the idea that a stock always has 2 prices, the bid price and the ask price.

BID PRICE = This is the price where you will **sell** the stock

ASK PRICE = This is the price you will **buy** the stock and what sellers are willing to get for it

The spread is where you lose right away and the broker makes money off of you .You are essentially always losing on the initial entry of the trade because of the costs associated with the trade. This doesn't mean you will lose money on the trade all together you just have to be very conscious of how costs effect the profitability of a trade.

ECN/ROUTING COSTS

ECN and routing fees are charged on a per-share cost basis. Each broker has their own unique structure in how these are accessed. These costs are usually really small but it is good to mention them. These are fees charged to route your trades to the exchanges. They typically range anywhere from $.003 per share to $.005 or more.

DATA FEED COSTS/ PLATFORM COSTS

These are going to vary from broker to broker and some brokers will have no data feeds costs or platform costs. Majority of professional traders will use a fast data feed and highly dependable platform. They also vary depending on what type of instrument you plan to trade. Data feed costs can start at $50 and go all the way up to a few thousand. Platform costs can also be that high.

Most retail brokers will offer platforms and data feeds for their clients for free. Some of the time though the free versions can have delayed pricing and execution. Not always but it is possible. You get what you pay for. The paid data feeds and platforms will typically have a dedicated account rep or staff delegated to them. They will also have backups in place in case pricing goes down. This is for top-tier traders and institutions.

I suggest you keep your costs low and start with a free version. Below are the top 3 stock brokers to use in terms of cost, execution and customer service.

- **Interactive brokers**
- Best in terms of pricing/execution
- Sub-par customer service
- Best for experienced traders
- https://www.interactivebrokers.com/en/home.php

- **Scott-Trade**
- Great customer service
- Solid execution
- Great for beginners
- https://www.scottrade.com/

- **TD Ameritrade**
- Great pricing and execution

- Excellent Customer service
- Great for beginners and advanced traders
- https://www.tdameritrade.com/

If you plan to open a trading account I highly recommend the three above. However you should also do your own research because you may come across a broker that suits your specific needs better.

OPTIONS

Introduction

You may have heard the term options before but like most people you may be wondering what the heck are they and how do they work? Options are a very powerful and dynamic trading instrument. They offer different ways to hedge your risk in any market environment.

Options can be very low risk or very high risk depending on your risk appetite. Options trading can happen in many different security markets and can involve different instruments from stocks, stock indexes, exchange traded funds, fixed income products, foreign exchange and even commodities.

What are Options?

- Options are contracts that give the owner the right but not the obligation to buy or sell an underlying asset at a specific price on or before a specified future date
- They are traded in contracts so they can be traded for a single contract or several
- Just like a stock or a bond an option is a binding contract with defined terms and properties
- Options are derivatives, the value of options are derived from the value of their underlying asset
- Options can be traded in different security markets between different market participants including institutional investors, professional traders, hedge-funds, mutual funds and many others

Example of Options

You have been looking to purchase a house and have finally came across one that you want to buy but you won't have enough money to buy it for another 3 months. You talk to owner and strike a deal that gives you an **"option"** to buy the house in 3 months for $250,000. You and the owner agree and for this option you pay a price of $5,000.

Consider the following scenario's during the 3 months

1) During the 3 months you discover that the house belonged to a famous actor. As a result, the value of the house jumps to $500,000. Since the owner sold you the **"option"** he is obligated to sell you the house for $250,000. You decide to sell the house in the end and end up making a profit of $245,000 ($500,000 - $250,000 - $5,000).

2) While inspecting the house you discover that there is significant mold all around the house and that there is structural damage that can cause the house to collapse any day. Now you begin to re-evaluate the decision to purchase the house in the future, because you deem in worthless. Since you bought an **"option"** you are under no obligation to buy the house after the 3 months. You lose the $5,000 from the option, but you don't have to buy the house.

This example shows you that options are a right and not an obligation. It also shows you that you can let options expire worthless and lose 100% of your investment.

OPTION BASICS: CALLS & PUTS

In the jargon of options, contracts fall into two categories – calls and puts. A **CALL** represents the right of the holder to **BUY** a particular stock. A **PUT** represents the right of the holder to **SELL** a particular stock. Options use terminology that an investor should understand before buying or selling an option.

CALL OPTIONS

A call option is a contract which gives the buyer the right, but not the obligation to purchase shares of an underlying equity at specified price **(strike price)** within a fixed period of time **(expiration).** The seller of a call option is under contract to sell the underlying security if the buyer exercises his or her right to buy the option on or before the expiration date.

The **expiration** is the date on which an option contract automatically expires, or the last day an option may be exercised. For the writer (seller) of a call option it represents an obligation to sell the security at the strike price if the option is exercised. The call option writer is paid a premium for taking the risk.

The **strike price** is the price at which the underlying asset is bought or sold when the option is exercised. The strike price affects the **"money-ness"** of the option and it's the primary determent of the option's premium.

The options **premium** is the amount the buyer has to pay the option seller for carrying the risk on the option. The premium depends on the volatility of the security, strike price and expiration.

Visual interpretation of a call option (Long Call)

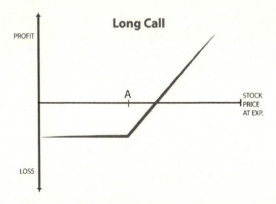

Since options contracts are a wasting asset they expire after a certain period of time. Once an option contract expires the right to exercise the option is gone and the option is worthless. The expiration month is specified on each option contract and it depends on the type of option.

Breaking Down a Call Option

"XYZ April 50 Call $12.50"

The option above contains five parts: "XYZ", "April", "50", "Call", and "$12.50".

XYZ – This represents the stock symbol for the underlying stock option contract.

April- This is the expiration date of the option contract. It is the day that the option contract expires. Typically, the expiration date of an option contract is the Saturday after the third Friday of each month.

50 – This is the strike price of the option contract. This is the price at which the buyer of the option contract may buy the underlying stock if the option contract is a call, or sell the stock if the option contract is a put.

Call – Indicates that type of option that is being used. In this example it's a call option.

$12.50 – This number is the premium or the price per share you pay to purchase the option contract. An option contract generally represents 100 shares of the underlying stock.

PUT OPTIONS

A put option is a contract which gives the buyer the right, but not the obligation to sell a specified number of shares of an underlying security at specified price **(strike price)** within a fixed period of time **(expiration).**

For the seller of the put option it's an obligation to buy the underlying security at the strike price if the buyer decides to exercise the option. The seller of the option (writer) is paid a premium for taking the risk associated with the option. Sellers of options are known as writers.

Visual Interpretation of a Put Option (Long Put)

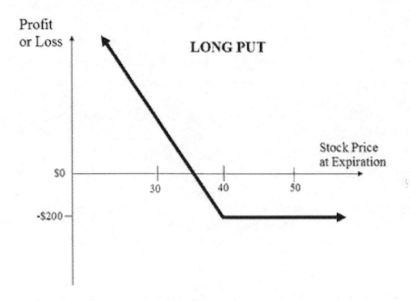

Breaking Down a Put Option

"XYZ May 90 Put $20.75"

The option above contains five parts: "XYZ", "May", "90", "Put", and "$20.75".

XYZ – This represents the stock symbol for the underlying stock option contract.

May- This is the expiration date of the option contract. It Is the day that the option contract expires. Typically, the expiration date of an option contract is the Saturday after the third Friday of each month.

90 – This is the strike price of the option contract. This is the price at which the buyer of the option contract may buy the underlying stock if the option contract is a call, or sell the stock if the option contract is a put.

Put – Indicates that type of option that is being used. In this example it's a put option.

$20.75 – This number is the premium or the price per share you pay to purchase the option contract. An option contract generally represents 100 shares of the underlying stock.

Money-Ness: Breakdown

Before we fully break down strike prices in relation to the options premium it is important to understand what the money-ness of an option is. Money-ness describes the relationship between the strike price of an option and the current trading price of the actual security. There are 3 terms that describe the money-ness of options: In-the-money (ITM), Out-of-the-Money (OTM), and At-the-Money (ATM).

ITM: In-the-Money

- Call option = ITM when the strike price is lower than the current price of the underlying security
- Put Option = ITM when the strike price is higher than the current price of the underlying security
- ITM options are more expensive because their premiums have higher intrinsic value on top of their time value.

OTM: Out-of-the-Money

- Call option = OTM when the strike price is higher than the current price of the underlying security
- Put option = OTM when the strike price is lower than the current price of the underlying security

Page52

- OTM options have zero intrinsic value. They are cheaper and their premium is only time value. They have a high chance of expiring worthless.

ATM: At-the-Money

- Call Options & Put Options = ATM when the strike price is equal to the market price of the underlying security
- ATM options have no intrinsic value and only contain time value which is highly influence by the overall volatility of the instrument and time.

Strike Price: Breakdown

So we know that the strike price is the price at which the underlying asset is bought or sold when the options is exercised, but what other factors does in affect? When analyzing which options are best to buy and sell the options premium and money-ness depend on the options strike price.

Strike Price & Call Options Price

There is a direct relationship between the strike price and the call option price. The higher the strike price of an option the cheaper the option will be. The table below illustrates this relationship by showing the options premiums for near term call options at different strike prices when a stocks is trading at $50.

Strike Price	Money-ness	Call Option Premium	Intrinsic Value	Time Value
35	ITM	15.5	15	0.5
40	ITM	11.25	10	1.25
45	ITM	7	5	2
50	ATM	4.5	0	4.5
55	OTM	2.5	0	2.5
60	OTM	1.5	0	1.5
65	OTM	0.75	0	0.75

Strike Price & Put Options Price

There is also a direct relationship between the strike price and the put option price. The higher the striker price the more expensive the option will be. The table below illustrates this relationship by showing the options premiums for near term put options at different strike prices when a stock is trading at $50.

Strike Price	Money-ness	Call Option Premium	Intrinsic Value	Time Value
35	OTM	0.75	0	0.75
40	OTM	1.5	0	1.5
45	OTM	2.5	0	2.5
50	**ATM**	**4.5**	**0**	**4.5**
55	ITM	7	5	2
60	ITM	11.25	10	1.25
65	ITM	15.5	15	0.5

Options Premium Broken Down

So we know that the options premium is the amount the buyer has to pay the options seller for carrying the risk on the options. It depends on the volatility of the security, strike price and expiration. But what are the two parts that create the options premium? The options premium consists of two parts: the intrinsic value and time value.

Intrinsic Value
The intrinsic value is simply the difference between the current market price of an instrument and the strike price. From our money-ness breakdown earlier we know the only options that have intrinsic value are ITM options.

Intrinsic Value = (Current Market Price – Strike Price)

Example

A call options strike price = $25
The current stock's price = $40

Intrinsic value of the call option = $15

Time Value

The time value of an option depends on how much time is remaining to exercise the option, the money-ness and also the volatility of the instrument. The time value of an option goes down as it gets closer to its expiration date. It becomes worthless after the expiration date. This creates the concept of time decay in options, coining them as **"wasting assets"**.

The time value on ITM options is calculated by subtracting the intrinsic value from the options price. As the option goes more and more into the money the time value decreases. OTM options have no intrinsic value so in their case the time value is equal to the options price.

Expiry

Stock options in the United States expire on the 3rd Friday of the current expiration month. The only time that they don't expire on a Friday is if Friday happens to be a U.S. holiday. Before beginning to trade options you should look at the options expiration calendar. It shows you a current schedule of upcoming expiration dates for stock options. Below is the link.

http://www.optionsclearing.com/about/publications/expiration-calendar-next-year.jsp

List of the top 5 options brokers

- Options-Xpress (http://www.optionsxpress.com)
- Trade-Station (http://www.tradestation.com)
- EOption (http://eoption.com)
- TD Ameritrade (https://www.tdameritrade.com)
- Options-House (https://www.optionshouse.com)

FUTURES

BRIEF HISTORY OF FUTURES

In the 1840's, Chicago was becoming the mecca of the commercial exchange with railroads and telegraph lines connecting through it. In 1848 the Chicago Board of Trade was formed which gave birth to the futures contract. The very first futures contracts were created for commodities, specifically agricultural commodities.

If you have ever read about futures the typical story-line about them is that they were created to help farmers hedge against the price-fluctuations of the crops that they produced. Futures can be a great way to hedge specific market risk and they can also be used for regular trading and speculation. Futures are a leveraged product which can help traders reap huge profits, but also carries a significant risk.

The first futures contract that was ever traded was for corn. After that it was followed by wheat, soybeans, cotton, cocoa, orange juice, sugar, pork cattle and many others. Contracts for other products slowly began to develop. By the 1970's futures trading began to penetrate other markets.

THE FUTURES CONTRACT

A futures contract is an agreement, a legal agreement at that, to buy or sell a specific instrument at a preset price at a specific time in the future. The underlying asset for a futures contract could be stocks, commodities, currencies, bonds and other instruments. The terms of a futures contract are standardized in quantity and the delivery date. The exchanges facilitate the trading between buyers and sellers. In order to trade futures traders need to obviously put up cash, which is commonly referred to as margin in futures trading. Proper margin must be maintained for the life of the trade.

MARGIN

Traders need to have sufficient margin in order to trade futures. This will usually depend on the kind of future that is being traded and how many contracts. In order to fully understand margin there are 3 different types of margin to understand.

- Initial Margin
- Clearing Margin
- Maintenance Margin

Initial Margin

The initial margin is the amount that is required to execute a futures trade. This amount is typically set and facilitated by the exchanges themselves. The real exposure of the trade can be greater than the initial margin. If the loss of a trade becomes greater than the initial margin it may prompt a margin call by the broker. If a broker issues a margin call traders are expected to post margin to bring the account back up that day. Majority of futures accounts are **"marked to market"** daily by brokers. This means that futures contracts are re-evaluated at the end of each trading day. The profit and loss are added and subtracted from the margin on a daily basis.

Example of Initial Margin

Initial margin for futures is set by the exchanges and this amount usually varies anywhere from 5%-15% of the contract. This can also vary from broker to broker. Let's use the following example.

A trader wants to get into a wheat contract for $50,000 and the initial margin percentage is set to 10% for wheat futures contracts.

The initial margin amount the trader would need to post is only $5,000. The important thing to note about the initial margin is that it can be subject to change by the exchanges if volatility picks up.

Clearing Margin

Clearing Margin is money that is required for brokerages and institutional firms to have on hand to complete futures transactions with their clients. It is a form of capital protection for brokers to have in order to ensure client trades are executed.

Maintenance Margin

The maintenance margin is the minimum amount of cash a trader must maintain in their account to keep a trade open for a futures contract. If the net value of the account falls below the maintenance margin it will prompt the broker to issue a margin call. Once a margin call is issued the trader must post more funds to bring the account value above to the minimum.

SETTLEMENT IN FUTURES

When a trader enters into a futures position he or she has 4 different options as to how they can settle the trade.

- Straight Cash Settlement
- Physical Delivery
- Expiration
- Regular Closeout

Straight Cash Settlement

Once the futures contract expires the parties to the transaction pay or receive cash for the transaction. This is most common when a certain future doesn't have an option for physical delivery.

Physical Delivery

Physical delivery is extremely uncommon today. Less than 1% of futures contracts actually take physical delivery of the underlying asset. If it does happen the amount specified in the contract is delivered by the seller of the contract to the actual exchange. It can happen with commodities but it's very rare.

Let's say for example you had 1 contract on wheat futures. The standard contract size for wheat futures is 5000 bushels. When the contract expires you can take physical delivery of 5000 bushels of wheat. Even though most brokers will only do cash settlements it is worth to note that there is a very small percentage that takes physical delivery. I don't know about you but I prefer cash over wheat any day.

Expiration

The expiration date of a futures contract is when that futures contract stops trading and gets the final settlement price for that specific period. Most brokers typically expire a trader's position by closing their trade out and giving them the option to re-open it for the new contract month and at the new contract price.

Regular Closeout

This is the most common closeout. A trader simply closes out their futures position at the current market price. A lot of day traders use a regular closeout and typically don't hold long term positions up until expiry for futures.

DIFFERENT TYPES OF FUTURES CONTRACTS & CODES

A futures contract can technically be created on anything. All you really needs is two different counterparties to create the transaction. They don't necessarily have to happen through the facilitation of an exchange. It is best to trade futures that are actually facilitated and standardized by an official exchange. Since futures are a standardized contract they have specific symbol structure and abbreviations. Futures contracts can be traded on the following markets.

- Agricultural
- Currencies
- Equity Index
- Financial
- Meats/Dairy
- Metals
- Softs

It is important to make note of some of the futures codes and abbreviations that you might see on your trading platform. Knowing what these are is important in order to keep track of your margin and what contract month is actually trading. Below are the abbreviations for each contract month.

- F= January
- G= February
- H = March
- J= April
- K=May
- M=June
- N=July
- Q= August
- U=September
- V= October
- Z= December

The link below is for a good futures broker and their current futures offering. This link shows you the current futures and their designated symbols along with their current session trading times.

https://www.lightspeed.com/futures/

Let's take the following example. Let's say you wanted to view the current price of Natural Gas futures for this current month (January) and current year (2016).

The symbol code for this would be **NGF6.**

NG = symbol abbreviation for Natural Gas (symbol abbreviations can be found at the link above)
F= is the current contract month
6= the last digit of the 2016 expiration year

Getting familiar with how contracts work is important before beginning to trade them. It is also very important to remember when certain futures contracts expire before actually beginning to trade them. Futures contracts are very risky trading instrument but can be the fastest and most liquid instrument to trade. Futures contracts tend to have great liquidity, low spreads and predictable volatility.

CHAPTER 4

FOREX

Forex stands for the foreign exchange market, or currency trading market. The forex market is known as **"decentralized"** market because trades are done off an exchange. The currency trading market is the largest market in the world. The forex market yields a whopping $5.6 trillion dollars a day in trading volume. This is massive when compared to the $25 billion per day volume on the New York Stock Exchange.

So what is forex? If you have ever went to a different country there is typically a currency exchange kiosk directly at the airport. Let's say you are taking a trip from the United States to Great Britain and once you land you need to exchange your money from dollars to pounds. The exchange rates are published on the boards and you hand over your dollars and receive back pounds. You have just performed a currency transaction.

Instruments Traded In Forex

Forex trading or currency trading is just the trading of different countries money. You are not owning a stock or a futures contract. You are essentially just trading money back and forth. The exchange rate of one currency compared to another is a direct reflection of that country's economic health versus the other. Let's take a look at the top major currencies traded.

- USD = United States   >>> (US-Dollar)
- EUR= Euro   >>> (Euro)
- GBP= Great Britain   >>> (Great Britain Pound)
- JPY= Japan   >>> (Japanese-Yen)
- CHF= Switzerland   >>> (Swiss-Franc)
- NZD= New Zealand   >>> (Kiwi)
- CAD= Canada   >>> (Canadian-Dollar)
- AUD= Australia   >>> (Aussie)

Symbols are always abbreviated by 3 letters. The currencies above are considered the majors because they tend to have the highest volume.

Currency trading is done and facilitated by a **"forex"** broker. It is done by trading currency pairs against each other. Below is a list of the major **"currency pairs"** and their nicknames.

Pair	Countries	Nickname
EUR/USD	Eurozone/US	Euro-Dollar
GBP/USD	Great Britain/US	Pound-Dollar
USD/JPY	US/Japan	Dollar-Yen
USD/CAD	US/Canada	Dollar-Cad
NZD/USD	New Zealand/US	Kiwi-Dollar
AUD/USD	Australia/US	Aussie-Dollar
USD/CHF	US/Switzerland	Dollar-Swiss

If you notice all the majors contain the US dollar. There are also other combinations of crosses that you can trade that start with each major currency. These are commonly referred to as the **"minor pairs"**, or **"cross-pairs"**. Below is a list of the cross pairs.

Euro Cross Pairs

Pair	Countries	Nickname
EUR/GBP	Euro/Great Britain	Euro-Pound
EUR/CHF	Euro/Switzerland	Euro-Swiss
EUR/CAD	Euro/Canada	Euro-Cad
EUR/AUD	Euro/Australia	Euro-Aussie
EUR/NZD	Euro/New Zealand	Euro-Kiwi

Pound Cross Pairs

Pair	Countries	Nickname
GBP/AUD	Great Britain/Australia	Pound-Aussie
GBP/CAD	Great Britain/Canada	Pound-Cad
GBP/NZD	Great Britain/New Zealand	Pound-Kiwi
GBP/CHF	Great Britain/Switzerland	Pound-Swiss

Yen Cross Pairs

Pair	Countries	Nickname
EUR/JPY	Euro/Japan	Euro-Yen
GBP/JPY	Great Britain/Japan	Pound-Yen
CAD/JPY	Canada/Japan	Cad-Yen
CHF/JPY	Switzerland/Japan	Swiss-Yen
NZD/JPY	New Zealand/Japan	Kiwi-Yen
AUD/JPY	Australia/Japan	Aussie-Yen

There are many cross combinations available. The ones above are the most common. It is also important to mention some less traded and higher volatility pairs known as the **"exotics"**. Exotic currencies are currencies of developing countries. These types of crosses tend to have very wide spreads and high swap interest payments. Below are just a few of the exotic currency pairs.

Pair	Countries	Nickname
USD/SEK	US/Sweden	Dollar-Seki
USD/DKK	US/Denmark	Dollar-Krone
USD/TRY	US/Turkey	Dollar-Lira
USD/ZAR	US/South Africa	Dollar-Rand

The forex market is comprised of hedge funds, retail brokers, liquidity providers, global banks and institutional traders. Unlike the stock market the forex market is open **24/5**. Trading begins on Sunday at 5p.m and stays open without a session close until Friday at 5p.m. Most people that trade forex use a retail broker. Only a few individual traders will utilize direct market trading with a large institution because the minimum capital deposit tends to be very high. Below are few of the most popular retail forex brokers.

- FXCM
- Oanda
- LMAX
- Alpari
- Hot-Forex
- FX-Open

- Think-Forex
- JFD-Brokers
- Forex.com

The most popular way that forex is traded is directly through the spot market. There are also alternative ways to trade currencies. Some include through the use of futures contracts, options and ETF's. Foreign exchange trading is unlike any other trading due to its overall flexibility and versatility. Below are some advantages of trading forex.

- Low Commission or no commission structure (some brokers don't charge commissions)
- Flexible trade sizes
- 24/5 market
- High leverage (some brokers can give you leverage as high as 1000:1)
- Constant volatility
- High Volatility
- High bonus and rebate structure with brokers

How are exchange rates determined? Foreign exchange rates are determined by the major banks in the world. This can be very good for traders because the price of a currency has a very low chance of being moved by 1 significant high volume trader.

Forex Session Times

Before beginning to trade forex you should be aware of the four major trading sessions. Each session brings in their own unique volatility.

- London Session   EST (3:00 AM – 12 PM)
- New York Session   EST (8:00 AM – 5:00 PM)
- Sydney Session   EST (4:00 PM - 1:00 AM)
- Tokyo Session   EST (6:00 PM- 3:00 AM)

Once a certain session opens up for trading volatility in that specific currency tends to pick up. The busiest trading session out of the four mentioned is the London session. As a forex trader you want to trade the session and day of the week the presents the best volatility.

Ideal Trading Time

- **Middle of the week** (Wednesday- Friday). These days tend to have the highest average daily pip movements of the week.
- **During Session Opens.** Volatility and pip movement during session opens and session overlaps tends to be the highest.

Times to Avoid Trading

- Major bank holidays – lower market movements and wider spreads
- News Events- risk of trading is higher and spreads can be extremely wide
- Friday after 12:00 p.m. – Liquidity decreases drastically and the market moves very slow

Forex Trade Example

In forex trading money is made the same way in any other market, by buying and selling. In a forex trade you want to buy a certain currency in the anticipation that the price will go up and sell in an anticipation that it will go down.

Example Trade

Trade: Trader buys 20,000 Euros at EUR/USD rate of 1.9000
   1 Week later the EUR/USD rate has jumped to 1.2000
    The Trader closes the trade out for a $2,000 profit

Calculation: 20,000 X 1.90 = $38,000
     20,000 X 2.00 = $40,000
Profit: **$2,000**

Commonly Used Forex Lingo

What does a **PIP** stand for in forex? PIP stands for **Percentage in Points**. In forex pips are the unit of measurement to illustrate the change in price of a currency. For example if GBP/USD rate is currently at **1.4501** and it moves to **1.4502**, this would illustrate a one pip move. Most brokers quote forex pairs to the 4th decimal place but some can go to five. Forex also has different sizing depending how much you want to trade.

The specific trading sizes in forex are called **lots**. Below are the different lot increments.

- 1 Standard Lot = 100,000 units
- 1 mini Lot = 10,000 units
- 1 micro lot = 1,000 units
- 1 nano lot = 100 units

As a forex trader you should be aware of the maximum **leverage** that a broker is willing to give you and what you current account leverage is before you start trading. The most leverage that a US broker will give you is 50:1. Other foreign brokers can go as high as 1000:1.

Let's use this example to illustrate leverage in forex.

Your current account leverage is set to 100:1 and you currently have $5,000 in your trading account. You want to open a position for $100,000. Since you have 100:1 leverage you have no problem with opening this trade. The margin requirement for this trade is only 1%. Forex trading tends to be very highly leveraged market.

In order to be a successful forex trader it is important to only trade at specific market hours and trade only highly liquid pairs. The best way to get an idea of how the forex market moves is to open a demo account and practice trading. Every single forex brokers will allow you to open a demo account. There are typically no platform fees with forex trading.

By trading a demo account for a few weeks with virtual funds you can begin to develop a sense of when and how prices move. You will also begin to see when to avoid trading and how each session times affect one another.

ETF'S

What the heck are ETF's? Many of us have probably never even heard of these trading instruments. An ETF stands for an **"Exchange-Traded Fund"**. An ETF is a grouped basket of securities that track a particular asset class that you can buy and sell. They are offered on many different markets. Below are some of the markets that ETF's are offered on.

- Index ETF's
- Equity ETF's
- Bond ETF's
- Commodity ETF's

ETF STRUCTURE

An ETF typically represents a fund or a company that has direct ownership in different assets and splits the ownership into shares. Like a regular stockholder you are entitled to share in interest earnings and dividends. ETF's can be owned long term like a stock and also day traded which makes them an extremely attractive investment. They are most similar to mutual funds. The number of shares outstanding for ETF's changes on a daily basis because new shares are created daily and existing shares are redeemed.

Creation units

Creation units are large blocks of ETF shares that are then traded for mix of the underlying securities. The creation units make up the actual fund. Creation units are a must for the ETF because they essentially create the liquidity in the underlying asset class.

Redemption

Redemption refers to the method of how ETF's are reconciled from their net asset value and the current market value when they are traded.

PROS of ETF'S

- Ability to trade actively
- Lower Commissions

- Reduction in capital gains tax
- Highly liquid
- Transparent

CONS of ETF'S

- Pricing issues, allows for plenty of arbitrage
- Settlement, ETF's have 3 day settlement period
- Thin Liquidity, some ETF's can have high spreads

INDEX ETF's

Index ETF's try to mimic the overall performance of an index. These can be based on many different instruments or asset classes. Below are some of the most commonly known Index ETF's.

- SPIDER ETF (SPY) – tracks the performance of the S&P 500 Index
- IWM – tracks the performance of the Russell 2000 Index
- QQQ – tracks the performance of the Nasdaq 100
- DIA- tracks the performance of the Down Jones Industrial Average

EQUITY ETF'S

Equity ETF's can be broken down between different cap sizes. They can track equities with small-caps, mid-caps and large-caps. Equity ETF's can also track a specific sector of the economy. This is great for people that want to invest their money into a trending industry.

BOND ETF'S

Bond ETF's are funds for different type of government bonds. They can be regular treasury bonds and bonds issued by financial institutions.

COMMODITY ETF's

Commodity ETF's can be funds that track the overall performance of different types of commodities or even a mixture of commodities in a similar class. Below are a few examples.

- Metals (Gold, Silver, Platinum, Palladium)
- Energy/Oil
- Meats, Cattle
- Softs, Food and Fiber
- Grains

Trading ETF's is a lot like trading an equity. You can use different market orders and trade as much as your heart desires. They don't have minimums. They are also very interesting because you can also trade options on them but that is beyond the scope of this book.

BONDS

For most people bonds tend to be the most boring instrument of all. What is a bond? A bond is debt. If you are investing in bonds you should begin to look at it as you loaning money to a company or entity. Bonds are used to raise money and finance projects and operations of companies. Investors of bonds are typically known as creditors or debtholders. Bonds of public corporations, private corporations and government entities are traded on the exchanges. There are only a select few that are traded over the counter.

If a company needs to raise money for new projects, expand current operations, or to clean up their current debt, they issue bonds. The institutions that issue the bonds owe the holders of the bond interest and principal that must be paid back at a future date. Bonds have unique features that investors and traders should be aware of before deciding to trade or invest. They are listed below

- Principal
- Coupon rate
- Yield rate
- Maturity
- Credit Rating
- Market Price

PRINCIPAL

The principal amount is also known as the face amount. It is the total amount that the interest is paid on by the issuer. This amount has to be repaid at the end of the term of the bond.

COUPON RATE

This is the interest rate that the issuer is entitled to pay to the bond holder. This is usually a fixed interest rate. Interest payments on bonds can be made in different intervals. They can be monthly, Semi-annually or annually.

YIELD RATE

This is the rate of return which is received from investing in the bond. The yield rate can refer to two things: the current yield or the YTM **(yield to maturity).**

Current yield

The current yield is the sum of the annual interest payments divided by the market price of the bond.

Yield to Maturity

The yield to maturity is the total return which is projected on a bond if the investor or trader holds it until the maturity date. It is also commonly referred to as the **IRR (internal rate of return).**

Internal Rate of Return

The IRR is a measurement that is meant to project the profitability of a specific investment.

MATURITY

The company or institution that "issued" the debt (bond) is entitled to pay the amount on the maturity date. At the maturity date all the principal and interest are paid back. Bonds tend to be a longer term investment vehicle and most bonds tend to have a term anywhere from 5-30 years. There are however, short term bonds, mid-term bonds and long term bonds. Each will tend to have a slightly different structure.

CREDIT RATING

The credit rating of a bond is a grade that is given to a bond to indicate the probability of repayment on the bond. They are also meant to identify the overall risk associated with the bond. Below are the top 3 rating agencies in the United States

- Standard and Poor's (S&P)
- Moody's
- Fitch Group

Bond ratings are illustrated with letters starting from "AAA" being the highest. Below are the different bond ratings.

The A Graded Bonds

- High-Grade prime bonds
- Low investment risk
- Very high chance of full repayment

Different A bond rated Variations

- AAA, AA+, AA, AA-, A+, A, A-

The B Graded Bonds

- Lower-Grade bonds
- Slight Investment Risk
- Chance of loss or default

Different B bond rated Variations

- BBB+, BBB, BBB-, BB+, BB-, B+, B, B-

The C Graded Bonds

- Low Grade bonds
- High risk of default
- Higher interest rates

Different C Bond rated Variations

- CCC+, CCC, CCC-, CC+, CC-, C+, C, C-

The D Graded Bonds

- Garbage/ junk Bonds
- Very high interest rate
- High probability of default or already in default

Different D Bond rated Variations

- DDD, DD, D

MARKET PRICE

The price of the bond is influenced by all the factors above. This price will fluctuate during the life of the bond. The bond may trade at a discount or above market. You should be aware that when the price of a bond goes down the interest goes up and visa-versa.

There are many different types of bonds that a trader can utilize. Below is a small list of the different bonds you can trade.

- Junk Bonds (high-interest rate, high probability of default)
- Zero-Coupon Bonds (pay no interest, high discount)
- Convertible Bonds (can exchange for shares in the company that has issued the bond)
- Government Bonds (T-bonds, issues by the government, very low default risk)
- Municipal Bonds (Issued by a state, local government etc.)

Bonds have been a go-to safe haven investment for many people because they tend to carry very low investment risk. You should however be aware of the different types of bonds there are out there in case you have different idea on how you want to profit from them.

CHAPTER 5

PTD RULE

PTD stands for the Pattern Day trading rule. As defined by **FINRA** (Financial Industry Regulatory Authority) a **"pattern day trader"** is a trader who executes four or more **"day trades"** within five business days, if the number of day trades are greater than 6% of the customer's total net trading activity. Under FINRA rules and regulations, clients of brokers who are considered "pattern day traders" must have at a **minimum of $25,000** in their trading accounts. This rule essentially establishes that you have a minimum of $25,000 in order to day trade equities.

This rule is specific to equity trading only. This does not pertain to futures, forex, options, etc. It is important to note because if you were planning on day trading equities with less than $25,000 you are fairly limited in terms of the amount of trades you can execute. Other instruments such as futures, forex, options and others, have no limit. You can fire off trades left and right as long as you have enough margin in your account to support opening up a trade.

So why is this relevant to traders? If traders were not aware of this rule and they were day trading equities there could be some issues. The rule essentially limits you to 4 stock trades per week if you are trading with less than $25,000. For example, if you executed 4 trades so far this week and you need to close one of your positions the broker will most likely issue a reject until the 5 days are up.

This was enacted because regulators believed that traders or investors with less than $25,000 were considered less sophisticated and wanted to limit the "potential" loss on their accounts by putting on this regulatory minimum. Some people argue that this type of regulation is limiting the potential for further market liquidity in equities. Some will say it's helped many investors make their investments safer and less volatile. Regardless of the rationale behind this rule, it is important to be aware of capital limitations before one decides to day trade equities.

BASIC ORDER TYPES

Before eloping on your trading journey it is important to shed light on the different ways you can enter into trade. There are a plethora of sophisticated order types that are used by professional traders and institutions. We will go over the most basic orders types that are used by most retail and institutional traders. Below are the most basic order types and ones that you should become very familiar with before starting to trade.

- Market Orders
- Limit Orders
- Stop Orders
- Conditional Order Types
- Execution slippage <<< (not an order type, but result of an order)

MARKET ORDERS

The fastest and most basic form of an order is a direct market order. It is the fastest way to hop into a trade and the fastest way to get out of one. Market orders don't guarantee you the best possible fill price, instead they guarantee execution. It directs the broker to buy or sell at the current market rate. If you absolutely need to get out of a trade a market order is the best and quickest way to do so.

The only bad part about straight market orders is that price is not guaranteed, which can typically lead to execution slippage. In order to avoid execution slippage you should trade instruments that have high liquidity.

A market order to **"buy"** a certain instrument will be filled at the **"ask"** price. A market order to "sell" a certain instrument will be filled at the **"bid"** price.

LIMIT ORDERS

Limit orders are a great way to prevent a trade from getting execution slippage, however they do not guarantee a fill. A Limit order will be executed and filled only if the market price of an instrument reaches the pre-set limit price within the order. Limit orders can be very useful way to get into a trade at a price that you really want. There are two types of limit orders: a buy limit and a sell limit.

Buy limit – A buy limit order is an order to buy an instrument at or **BELOW** a specified price. Price is guaranteed but the fill is not.

Sell limit – A sell limit order is an order to sell an instrument at or **ABOVE** a specified price. It also does guarantee a fill but the price is not.

STOP ORDERS

Stop orders are a great way to lock in profits or limit losses for a trade once a price goes past a certain level. Like a limit order a stop order is a way to buy or sell a certain instrument once it reaches a pre-specified price, the stop price. Once the stop price is hit the stop order becomes a market order. Once the order becomes a market order it means that execution is guaranteed. This however leaves room for execution slippage. Below are the following types of stop orders.

Sell Stop – A sell stop order is an order to sell an instrument **BELOW** the current market price.

For example, if a trader sees that the current price of an instrument is at $90 and believes that the price will drop, the trader can enter a sell stop at $80. If the price of the instrument drops to $80, the broker will sell the instrument at the next price. This can help to limit losses or lock in profits.

Buy Stop – A buy stop order is an order to buy an instrument **ABOVE** the current market price.

For example, if a trader sees that the current price of an instrument is at $90 and believes that the price will go up, the trader can enter a buy stop at $90. If the price of the instrument goes up to $100 the broker will buy the instrument at the next price. This can also help to limit losses and lock in profits.

TRAILING STOPS

A trailing stop order is very unique type of order because it can shift. A trailing stop order is an order that can be set at defined price points away from an instruments current market price. It is meant to protect profitable positions and limit your loosing ones.

If you are in a long position and want to protect your profits once the trade is profitable you can set a trailing stop **"BELOW"** the instruments current market price. If you are in short position you would set your trailing stop **"ABOVE"** the current market price.

This nifty little order is meant to protect your profits once a trade begins to move in your favor. It will also limit your losses. This can be set at a percentage of the current market price of an instrument or at specific dollar increments. As long as your position continues to move in your favor the trailing stop will automatically adjust with it by the set amount.

For example, let's say you purchased some shares in Apple at $100 per share. You can enter a trailing stop order at 10% on the trade to protect your cash. If Apple falls by 10% the trailing stop will be executed and your loss will be limited to 10%. Let's say that Apple moved up by 18% in the past two weeks and you are hype about your gains, but you believe that Apple can easily have a pullback in price.

You are right and Apple moves down by 8% the next week. Your trailing stop would be triggered and your order would get closed .You are happy because you are walking away with a nice 10% gain. It's a good way to limit your losses and protect your profits while capitalizing on the upside potential of a stock moving in your favor.

CONDITIONAL ORDER TYPES

Conditional order types are also a very unique type of order. They are for the more advanced trader and can be a great way to capture market gaps and volatile price swings. Conditional order types are orders that have to meet specific preset criteria before executing. If they fail to meet the criteria they are automatically cancelled.

Conditional order types allow you to set specific order triggers once the price of an instrument moves up or down a certain amount, or trades a certain amount of volume. They can be used on any trading instrument. The top 3 conditional orders are listed below.

- One cancels another (OCA)
- One triggers another (OTA)
- One triggers two (OTT)

One- Cancels -Another (OCA)

In this order type you enter in two orders at the same time. If one is executed the other will be automatically cancelled. For example, you want to buy one of two instruments but not both at the same time. With this specific order you can do that. Once the first order is filled the second will automatically cancel.

One- Triggers- Another (OTA)

In this order type if one order is executed a second order is automatically submitted for execution. For example, you buy 500 shares of Apple and a second order is then automatically submitted to purchase either more shares of Apple or another instrument. These can be common in interest rate arbitrage trades.

One- Triggers Two- (OTT)

In this order type if one order is executed two more orders are automatically submitted for execution. Say you buy Apple at $100 per share, two more orders are automatically submitted to purchase Apple at different price points. They can be either lower or higher depending on how you set them. They can essentially be used as trailing stops.

EXECUTION SLIPPAGE

What is execution slippage? Slippage can occur when trading any instrument. It is the price difference between what a trader expects to get filled in at for a trade and what they actually get filled at. The quote price that you see does not guarantee that your order will get filled in at that price. Your trade can get filled in at a worse price **(negative slippage)** or at a better price **(positive slippage).** Slippage occurs when your original order is activated on a different price than you intended it to execute at. You can thank volatility for that.

Execution Slippage

Negative Slippage

Negative slippage happens when your order gets executed on a rate that was worse than your expected rate. The example above illustrates that. People tend to experience negative slippage during news events or times of extreme volatility.

Positive Slippage

Positive slippage happens when your order gets executed on a rate that was better than your original submitted rate. By the time your trade fills you actually receive a better rate then you originally requested.

Is it possible to avoid slippage? Markets are not perfect and unfortunately avoiding slippage is difficult and sometimes depends highly on what kind of instruments you trade and what kind of broker you use. Prices move so fast that most traders won't even notice when slippage does happen.

FIX PROTOCOL

What is FIX Protocol? FIX stands for Financial Information eXchange. It is the language of the global financial markets and is used by almost all buy side and sell-side firms, trading platforms and regulators to communicate and send trade related information across to each other. It was initiated in 1992, by Robert Lamoureux and Chris Morstatt to create a trading connection between Fidelity Investments and Salomon Brothers.

It was designed for institutional clients and broker-dealers. Before FIX, information was communicated over the phone, but Fidelity realized that this process could cause information to be lost and sent to the wrong end client. Their goal was to create a protocol which would standardize and improve order routing and trade processing between major exchanges and other counterparties.

Who Uses FIX?

- Almost every major stock exchange and investment bank
- Big time bond Dealers
- Large Institutional Traders
- Thousands of smaller investment firms and brokerages
- Largest Mutual Funds and Money Managers
- Market Makers and Liquidity Bridge Providers

The FIX Protocol language is made up of a large series of messaging specs used in trade communications. It was originally created to help equities trading in the pre-trade and trade environment. It is now experiencing large growth in the post-trade space supporting **straight-through-processing (STP)** from **indications of interest (IOI)** to allocations and confirmations. It has seen large growth in fixed income trading, foreign exchange trading and the derivatives market.

FIX operates around a standard, which is owned, maintained and developed by the FIX trading community and its supporting member firms. Major leading firms work together to ensure that the standard is progressing and continues to meet technology demands.

Benefits of FIX Protocol

- Decrease in cost and integration of internal and external processes
- Ease of connection to new trading partners
- Reduction in software and hardware costs needed for automation and scaling
- Increase in communication between users by having a standardized language
- Fix is open protocol, it brings all major players together
- Wide community support and software packages available

Fix Supported Trading Instrument

- Stocks, Bonds
- Futures, Spread Bets
- Forex
- Fixed Income
- Options
- Swaps

STP (Straight-through-processing)

Straight- through-processing (STP) is a trading functionality which enables companies to increase the speed at which they can process transactions. This is done by automatically enabling information that has been entered electronically to be sent from one party to the other without having to re-enter information. STP is a major paradigm shift from traditional **T+3 trading** to same-day settlement process. The functionality helps to decrease settlement risk by cutting the transaction-processing time, which in return increases the likelihood that trades or agreements are settled within the specified time.

In the forex market, STP brokers simply place your orders to the next counterparty. They are typically known as the LP (Liquidity Provider). Trades are passed through to the LP via a FIX Connection that is setup between the LP and the broker.

Benefits of STP

- Eliminates human error in processing transactions and trades
- Transactions take less time to manage and process
- Lower fee options for investors

Trade Settlements (T+1, T+2 and T+3)

Whenever you buy or sell any type of financial instrument there are always two dates which you should be aware of: trade date and the settlement date. The 3 abbreviations above T+1, T+2, T+3, refer to the settlement date of a particular security transaction.

T+1 stands for trade date plus 1 day, indicating when the security transaction will settle. Different markets have different settlements dates. Keeping track of all the settlement dates for many different instruments can become difficult. STP automates this process and makes settlement easy. Below are different settlement dates for different markets.

Securities and Settlement Periods	
Security Type	Settlement Date
Stocks	3 market days after trade date
Exchange-Traded Funds	3 market days after trade date
Forex	2 market days after trade date
Mutual Funds	1 market day after trade date
Options	1 market day after trade date

Indication of interest (IOI)

In the FIX trading community IOI's are single line messages which are sent from the dealer (sell-side) to the customer (buy-side).They are essentially a sales message sent from the broker dealer over FIX to customers indicating an interest to either buy or sell an instrument.

IOI's are known as a **"pre-trade"** message. There are primarily two types of IOI's. A generic, or otherwise known as a basic IOI, which contains the basic information for a transaction such as the instrument direction (buy/sell), and typically the volume. The other is a specific IOI which contains more information than a basic IOI and has a specific duration. Specific IOI's include specific price, number of shares or contracts, how long it's active for and the direction. Broker Dealers who issue these type of IOI's will almost always honor the price and volume set within them.

Example IOI

A dealer has two traders Trader A and Trader B. Trader A sends out an order or request to purchase 1000 shares of APPL. The dealer then sends out an IOI-ID to Trader B indicating "SELL APPL". If Trader B is interested they can send back a sell order for APPL referring IOI-ID of the dealer.

CHAPTER 6

RATIOS

Performance Based Ratios

ROA
- Return on assets measures the profitability of a company relative to its total assets

(Return on Assets) = *Net Income ÷ Total Assets*

ROE
- Return on Equity is how much net income is returned as a percentage of the overall shareholders' equity

(Return on Equity) = *Net Income ÷ Shareholders' Equity*

EPS
- A portion of a company's profit that is allocated for each outstanding share of stock

(Earnings per Share) = *(Net Income – Dividends on Preferred Stock) ÷ Average Outstanding Shares*

Profit Margin
- How much of money the company keeps in earnings

(Profit Margin) = *Net Income ÷ Net Sales*

PE Ratio
- Measures a company's share price relative to its EPS

(Price-Earnings Ratio) = *Market Value per Share/ Earnings per Share*

Gross Profit Margin
- Portion of money left over from Revenues after COGS

(Gross Profit Margin) = *(Revenue – Cost of Goods Sold) ÷ Revenue*
COGS= Cost of Goods Sold

Dividend Payout Ratio
- The percentage of earnings that gets paid out to shareholders in dividends

(Dividend Payout Ratio) = Dividends/Net Income

Book Value Per Common Share
- This is used to determine how safe it is to own a stock after all debt is paid out.

(Book Value Per Common Share) =
(Total Shareholders' Equity – Preferred Equity) ÷ Total Outstanding Shares

Activity Based Ratios

Inventory Turnover
- This ratio is important because it can give you an insight into how efficient a company is. It compares inventory to amount sold.

(Inventory Turnover) = COGS/ (Beginning Inventory + Ending Inventory) ÷2

Average Collection Period
- This ratio looks at how long it takes for a company to receive money in accounts receivable

(Average Collection Period) = (Days in the period measured × Average amount of accounts receivable) ÷ (Total amount of sales during the period measured)

Asset Turnover
- Used by quants to measure the overall operational performance of a company.

(Asset Turnover) = (Net Sales) ÷ (Net Assets)

Financing Based Ratios

Debt Ratio
- This one is simple. It just looks at a company's total debt relative to its total assets

(Debt Ratio) = *(Total Liabilities)* ÷ *(Total Assets)*

Debt/Equity Ratio
- The infamous debt to equity ratio aims to compare total liabilities to the total shareholder's equity.

(Debt to Equity) = *(Total Liabilities)* ÷ *(Shareholders' Equity)*

Liquidity Ratios

Working Capital
- This is simply the total difference between current assets and current liabilities

(Working Capital) = *(Current Assets – Current Liabilities)*

Interest Coverage
- This is used to measure the rate at which a company can pay the interest on their current debt.

(Interest Coverage) = *(Earnings Before Interest and Taxes)* ÷ *(Interest Expense)*

Indicators

Simple Moving Average (SMA)

- The simple moving average is an average that is derived by adding the closing price of an instrument for a number of pre-specified periods then dividing it by the total number of pre-specified periods.
- Commonly used SMA's include the 5-day 20-day, 50-day and 200-day. You can essentially break down price movements into different periods and look at how price behaved differently between each period. Simple moving averages can give you an idea of where support and resistance lies for a specific instrument.
- Since the SMA is a "moving average", old prices are dropped and as new prices come in which will in turn change the SMA. Below is an example of a SMA.

Example of a 5-day SMA

Closing Prices of The Coca-Cola Company (KO): **(42.74) (42.96) (42.53) (42.34) (42.10)**

(42.74 + 42.96 + 42.53 + 42.34+ 42.10) ÷ 5 = **42.53**

Relative Strength Index (RSI)

- The relative strength index is meant to show **"overbought"** or **"oversold"** situations in a specific instrument. Most RSI's are used on 14 – day time period. They are measured on a scale of 0 to 100. The highs are typically marked at 70 and the lows are marked at 30.
- When the price of certain instrument moves up for quickly, at a certain point it will be considered **"overbought"**. When the price of a certain instrument moves down very quickly, at a certain point it will be considered **"oversold"**.
- There can be cases in which an RSI can be extremely low or extremely high. Levels such as 80 and 20 and even 90 and 10. These are extreme situations and can often happen during news

announcements when price reacts violently to a news event such as unemployment rates, interest rate announcements, GDP data, earnings announcements, etc.

Example RSI

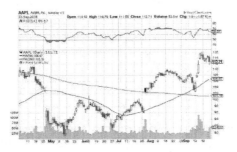

MACD

- The MACD stands for **"Moving Average Convergence Divergence"**. The MACD is one of the most simple and popular indicators used by traders. It is meant to identify trend and momentum. The MACD aims to show the convergence and divergence between two moving averages.
- The **"convergence"** happens when the two moving averages start approaching each other. The **"divergence"** happens when the two moving averages start moving away from each other.
- If the moving average period is shorter (12-day), the quicker the MACD price movements. If the moving average period is longer (26-day), the slower the MACD price movements.
- The MACD is calculated by using the differences between two moving averages. Below is a link that will show you how to calculate the MACD in Excel
- *http://investexcel.net/how-to-calculate-macd-in-excel/*
- The industry standard for MACD is the 12-day exponential moving average minus the 26-day exponential moving averages. The closing prices of an instrument are used to create the moving averages.
- The MACD depends on 3 different time parameters. The parameters are measured in days. The most common that traders tend to use

are 12, 26 and 9. You will most likely see them displayed in the
following way on your trading platform **MACD (12, 26, 9).** These are
meant to represent 2 weeks, 1 month and 1 and a half week.
- The "**signal line**" happens when the MACD and the average lines
  cross each other. The signal line is the 9-day exponential moving
  average of the MACD.

Example MACD

ADX

- ADX stands for average directional index. It is also commonly known
  as the average directional **movement** index. It is an indicator used
  to determine the strength of a trend in price for a specific
  instrument. It is meant to be used to identify strength only, not
  direction or momentum of price.
- The ADX will generate a signal once a certain price trend is already
  confirmed.
- The ADX has a standard range from 0 to 100. If the ADX is below 20
  that indicates that a certain trend in price is weak. If the ADX is
  above 40 this will indicate a strength in the trend. A trend that is
  really strong will be above 50.
- The ADX can be primarily used to screen instruments and confirm a
  certain trade. It is not used to generate buy or sell signals. It does
  however shed some light on where a certain instrument is with
  regards to its trend.

Example ADX

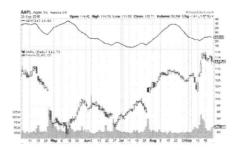

Stochastic Oscillator

- The stochastic oscillator is an indicator for identifying momentum and it is meant to show the location of the close for an instrument in relation to the high and low range over a pre-specified period of time.
- Since the stochastic oscillator is range bound, it can be very helpful in identifying where a certain instrument is overbought and oversold.
- The oscillator is not meant to follow price or volume, rather it is meant to measure the overall speed of a price movement.
- The industry standard for the stochastic oscillator usually defaults to 14 periods. The period range of 14 periods can be extended to days, weeks and months.
- The stochastic oscillator has a standard range from 0-100. Overbought instruments will use 80 as standard threshold and anything over 80 would typically be considered extremely overbought. Oversold instruments will use 20 as the standard threshold and anything under 20 would typically be considered extremely oversold. Below is a standard calculation for the oscillator and an example chart.

Example Calculation

= (Current Close price – Lowest Low price) ÷ (Highest High price – Lowest Low price) × 100

Lowest low price = lowest price of the analyzed period

Highest High price = highest price of the analyzed period

Example Chart

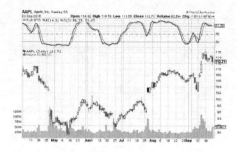

Types of Charts

Line Charts

- The line chart is the most basic type of chart in finance. There isn't much to it and it doesn't paint the most detailed picture of the price movement of an instrument.
- It is made by simply connecting a series of past prices together with a line on a graph.
- It can give you the most basic idea of where price is heading in general.
- Below is an example of a line chart.

Example Line Chart

Candlestick Charts

- Unlike a regular line chart, a candlestick chart will show you the open, high, low and close price of an instrument for a specific time period. This is powerful because it gives you a deeper view of how price behaved during certain period of time.
- It can show you how price moved during a bullish trend or a bearish trend.
- Below are the standard periods of time that a single candlestick can represent. Traders can customizes these as they see fit.

- 1 minute
- 5 minute
- 10 minute
- 15 minute
- 30 minute
- 1 hour
- 4 hour
- 8 hour
- 1 day
- 1 week
- 1 month

- There are many different ways that a certain candlestick can behave. Prices on candlesticks can be bullish, bearish, consolidating and ranging. Etc. To keep thing simple we will take a look at a standard bullish and bearish candle.

- Bullish candlestick

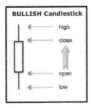

- Bearish Candlestick

- Let's take a look at what a standard candlestick chart looks like with each bar representing 1 day in price movement.

Example Candlestick Chart

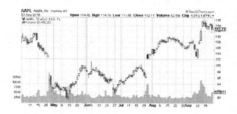

OHLC Charts

- The OHLC chart stands for open-high-low-close. This is essentially the same as a candlestick chart but it looks slightly different. See example below with each line representing 1 day in price.

Example OHLC Chart

- Each line on the chart illustrates the price range for that day. Below is an example of how an OHLC bar stacks up to a regular candlestick bar.

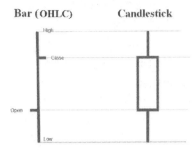

Bar (OHLC)   **Candlestick**

High

Close

Open

Low

-   The OHLC chart helps to visualize the price of an instrument with the same intention as a candlestick chart. They essentially show the same exact behavior in price. It is just a matter of personal preference to some to use the OHLC.

CONCLUSION

I applaud that you have decided to embark on this trading journey. Trading is a world of opportunity. It can be the quickest way to get rich and also the quickest way to lose all of your money. By developing a strong thirst for information you can succeed in trading. There is nothing stopping you from making a 1 million dollars or more from trading. Your only limitation is what you make it.

I hope this book has served you well and has given you the proper guidance and courage to begin trading.

Made in the USA
Lexington, KY
20 January 2017